M000035159

I Knew Them All by Heart

*The Legacy of a
Sunday School Teacher*

MYRTLE E. FELKNER

DISCIPLESHIP RESOURCES

PO BOX 340003 • NASHVILLE, TN 37203-0003
www.discipleshipresources.org

Cover design by Thelma Whitworth.
Interior design by PerfectType.

ISBN 0-88177-477-4

Library of Congress Control Number 2005934552

To the Teachers and Enablers with whom I learned

And

To the children who taught us how to teach.

Contents

$\mathcal{I}$ntroduction

I do not remember the first time I went to Sunday school, and have not yet come to the last time. I do remember how valued we felt as children in that little Danish-American church, and how I cherished my father's clear tenor voice rising in the Danish hymns he loved.

Our Sunday school superintendent blessed us with an uplifted hand each Sunday noon and, although I suppose we were expected to bow our heads, I still remember every line of Mr. Teusen's hand. When he blessed us, believe me, we were blessed.

And so I have been. For over sixty years I have taught children and youth in Sunday school and various other Christian education settings. Teachers who are willing to be flexible and vulnerable know that it is not enough to teach children the Ten Commandments and the books of the Bible. Our task is to meet the child where he or she is and to apply love, understanding, and Biblical truth to our relationships and to the class environment, so each child will feel beloved of God.

This book is not about methodology, although Sunday school teachers need to know that, too. This book is about learning—learning to be a Sunday school teacher, learning to teach as Jesus taught, learning the use of patience—until we see what makes the child tick and how to present Christian truths so each child will be open to Jesus.

Every Sunday school classroom should be a microcosm of the Kingdom of God. This can be difficult when you may have rebellious, angry, bored, excited, challenged, bright, active, intelligent, abused, or spoiled children—a cross section of the human condition, in other words. This book intends to help us recognize our possibilities as teachers in classrooms that include all those children.

I learned how to teach from these children. I remember and love them. They still have something to teach us. I want you to meet the children.

Although teaching children has always been my passion, this book is not about me, but about the children who taught me to teach. I have tried to pass on some of these insights in numerous workshops and other presentations. In the stories you will read here, I have often changed names or towns in order to spare anyone embarrassment. However, we recognize that we owe a debt of gratitude to the youngsters who have been so honest, so engaging, so frank and generous in sharing their life experiences.

Some of these children are now grown, with children of their own. Most, but not all, are individuals who attended the after-school ministries and the Sunday schools of a seven-church parish in the 70s, 80s, 90s, and indeed to the present time. We are grateful when we are able to tell the rest of the story, to record the impact Sunday school had in their lives, and to acknowledge the impact they have had upon the Christian education ministries of the church.

I Knew Them All By Heart is also one way of expressing appreciation to the children, and of acknowledging their contribution to our life in community. The implications for teaching and learning are clearly drawn from their life experiences.

Stacy

Stacy was a kindergartner when she first ventured across the street from the school to the church. She was a thin little child, with long bangs that grew over her eyes. Stacy had to give a good whiff to blow those bangs away long enough to give her shrewd and suspicious glance. Although she faithfully attended Monday school (an after-school program similar to Sunday school, but held on Mondays) for weeks on end, Stacy had a regimen, and she followed it faithfully.

"I hate you," she would declare, kicking her teacher in the shins.

"I'm sorry to hear that," answered her teacher, Thelma. "I love you, and God loves you."

This went on for weeks. One Monday in December, Stacy was late arriving. The children were in the sanctuary practicing their Christmas program when she came in the door, walked slowly down the middle aisle, whiffing away her bangs and inspecting each row of children. Finally, she found what she was seeking. Negotiating her way past the wiggly knees of her classmates, she came to our young minister. She climbed on his lap, leaned her head against his chest, and whiffed her bangs away one more time.

We blinked back tears at this first indication that Stacy was learning to trust her friends at church. Of course, things did not always go smoothly from then on. After all, Stacy was a rugged individualist, and so far in life that had stood her in pretty good stead.

I think Stacy was in third or fourth grade when I received my first letter from her. Whenever I could put my hands on extra take-home Sunday school papers, I sent them by mail to Stacy and other children. After all, it's fun to get your very own mail, along with a brief note. But Stacy's reply almost floored me:

> "Dear Myrtle—don't send no more papers. My daddy says they are too hard. Also, I hate Matthew and I hate Nancy and I hate you. Get out of my life. Love, Stacy."

Talk about mixed messages! I drove out to see Stacy, who lived in a small community not far from my home. Stacy and her mother greeted me cordially, and Stacy proudly showed me where her dad was putting up a partition wall so that she could have her very own room. Neither seemed to have any idea why Stacy had been so angry. "Just a bad day," guessed her mother.

Stacy followed me out to my car, dressed in her jeans and a thin little shirt. "Look, Myrtle," she shouted as I started to drive away. I rolled down the window and watched as she fell backwards into a snowdrift, then spread her arms in broad sweeps to make a snow angel. "It's for you," she declared.

I drove away, not particularly wiser, but at least not as worried.

Just before entering junior high, Stacy attended a church day camp. "Will you walk with me in the woods?" she asked. Stacy and I left the planned activities, following a path into the oak, walnut, maple, and hickory trees. We spoke little, enjoying the coolness of the timber, the quick scuttling of small animals, and the few birds overhead. In the middle of our stillness, Stacy said, "Myrtle, if someone jumps out from behind the bushes and tries to rape you, I'll run for help."

I thanked Stacy, sincerely and soberly. I knew that Stacy knew the world where rape happens better than I did, and Stacy knew that I knew that she knew that world. On that day, after all those years, Stacy and I trusted each other completely. I knew that I was safe when I walked in the woods with Stacy.

Stacy is grown now, married, with children of her own. Though she has had a tough time of it, Stacy earned her GED and has a job. She has stayed in the wider community.

Children are forever teaching me how to teach. Stacy's story has many implications for those of us engaged in a teaching ministry. Possibly the first one is patience. Stacy came early to our after-school ministry, just a kindergartner, but full of anger and defiance. Though she expressed this anger often and vehemently, her teachers were open to listen, faithful in expressing their love, and patient in dealing with her outbursts.

Stacy remembers her experience at Monday school, and although she and her family never became a part of our worshipping community, today Stacy says, "I have good memories. It laid a foundation for my family in later life. I belong to church, my children go to church, and now my parents go to church also."

First, without the patience of her church school teachers and pastors, this story might have been very different. For years, we walked with Stacy on her perilous life journey, and we learned that instant solutions to many problems are a pipe dream. Now Stacy tells us that she reads her Bible when she gets home from work, because in Monday school she learned "what God wants me to be." Patience is not a matter of an hour or so; it is the task of a lifetime. Never give up on a child. Never.

Second, Stacy demanded respect and got it. All children do not fit a certain preconceived mold, which is to say they are not wrong or less beloved by God. A paragon of virtue might make classroom management easier, and it certainly would have in Stacy's case, but the Stacys in our midst should be respected for who they are and what they can become. Good manners must be extended to all children, not just to the ones who fit the mold. Trust must be expressed repeatedly through both our actions and our words.

A Sunday school co-teacher once said to me, "We had better send the bad kids home so the class will be more peaceful and the good kids can learn something."

No way. There may be difficult children, angry children, or children with behavior problems, but there are no bad children. There are only children who need us to pray, guide, correct, love, respect, and stick with them. In return, they will teach us how to teach.

Josh

This little boy, blonde with the bluest eyes, was given away three times by the time he was three years old. His mother left her family when Josh was an infant. When the father could no longer care for the baby, he traveled to the mother's residence in another state and left him there. Before he turned three, his mother unceremoniously left him once again on his father's doorstep.

Everyone in town knew that, given half a chance, Josh would run away. He constantly wanted to go to far places to find his mother. His stepmother, in despair over this child who would not stay put, even made him a little harness and tied it with clothesline to an enormous tree in the yard. Josh played there with his tractors and trucks in the shade. When I first knew him, he was like a scared little rabbit, with nervous hands and wide, frightened eyes.

A school bus drove by the country church just a few blocks from Josh's home. The bus discharged several children at the church one day a week for an after-school children's Bible club. When Josh was in first grade, he often got off the bus, scurried to a ditch, and hid there until the bus had disappeared. No way was Josh going into that church!

Some days, I sat on the church steps reading a children's book until Josh crept out of the ditch to join me. I took him, with his stepmother's permission, for rides in the van. One day I asked if he would go into the church with me. He took my hand, but when we got to the door he put both hands imploringly on my shoulders and said, "Oh, Myrtle, let's not go in. I'm afraid of big people!"

A few weeks later, after we had read many books together, Josh and I stepped into the church and looked around. Josh saw children making things and listening to stories. But most of all, Josh heard one of the finest musicians in our community play the piano. He was fascinated with the music and said, "Myrtle, I might stay."

From then on, Josh came faithfully to Bible club. His job was to sit proudly on the piano bench with his teacher and turn the page when she said, "Now, Josh, please."

Josh still scampered away like a little rabbit on occasion. All through his growing-up years Josh told us repeatedly that someday he would find his mother.

Someplace along the line Josh lost his way. When a neighbor hired him to help clean a basement, he returned later to steal several items. He stole cigarettes in a grocery store, and when the manager confronted him, Josh pulled a knife. I was at his hearing, visited him in the county jail, and later visited the foster home where he was eventually placed. Josh often repeated his one desire: he wanted to see his mother.

Later, we learned that Josh had a son while still a teenager. He secured a job with a carpenter, and when his mother returned to the community to visit relatives, Josh got to see her. She rejected him soundly, and Josh bitterly asserted that he had never wanted to see her in the first place. Perhaps what looked like a petty crime wave all these years was really Josh's way of living out his frustration with life.

We have not been able to trace Josh, who by now is a young adult. Surely there is something we can learn from Josh's story?

Josh's family simply was not able to meet his needs. At a time of financial hardship, the church arranged for a

Christmas dinner to be provided for their large family. The following year, his father brought a generous check to the church with the request that it be used for Christmas dinner for another family with temporary hardships. These are people of good will and intent.

Perhaps the school, the church, and his parents all erred as we sought to help Josh. His problems were too deep, his loss too grievous. Josh needed early and intensive psychological help. Wherever Josh is now, our continual and fervent prayers accompany him.

Our hopes? Josh loved music and sang with a children's group in worship for two or three years. Those hymns and songs are forever etched in Josh's mind and memory, and our prayer is that he remembers the message and remembers the teacher for whom he turned the pages of the hymnbook.

Our hope and prayer is that Josh remembers the stories he loved to hear, that he remembers the week he spent at church camp, that he can chuckle over his excitement the first time he saw the entrance ramp to an interstate highway. We hope he recalls the cookies the ladies brought to church, and the games we played in that quiet little country churchyard. These memories just might give him the courage and the motivation to look again in his Bible, to sing again the music he loved, and to remember the teachers who have committed themselves to prayer on his behalf. We leave it to God.

Perhaps leaving it to God is the greatest lesson a teacher has to learn.

Three Sisters ✍

My husband and I, egged on by our children, had finally learned to ski. Though we had water-skied for years, this was a new adventure, and I quickly learned that I did not have the proper clothing for falling in the snow on a cold day. Hence, to the mall on a Saturday night I went.

I looked at the great variety of ski jackets: too expensive, too short, too long, too yellow, too dull, too many pockets. The only one I could even lean toward was yellow, and yellow is not a good color for me. I turned this way and that before the triple mirrors, trying to decide. Turning my head to catch a glimpse of my back in the mirrors, I spotted three little girls watching me intently—three little girls from Sunday school.

"Help me decide!" I urged my young friends, even as I was very much aware that they were dressed in thin jackets, totally insufficient for this frigid January.

"Turn around again," they urged. We tried the expensive one again, the short one, the long one, the dull one, and yes, they liked the yellow one best. All three assured me that I would always be warm and fine in the yellow jacket. I bought it.

That yellow ski jacket bothered me all weekend. By Monday morning I was on the phone asking several young mothers if they had any warm coats that their children had outgrown. By noon the trunk of my car was full of coats. After school, I drove to the home of my young friends.

"I have plenty of coats for your girls," I explained to their mother. "If it is okay with you, they may each have one coat for school and one for Sunday school." The delighted little girls carried the coats into the kitchen and began to try them on.

There was not a mirror in sight. Yet these children each put on a coat, then turned this way and that. They glanced over their shoulders. They tugged the coats down and zipped them up and zipped them down and turned this way and that again. My teacher's heart did a double take.

All these little girls knew about shopping for a coat, they had learned at the mall on Saturday night as their teacher picked out a ski jacket. They modeled the whole procedure, coat after coat, until each had one for school, and one for Sunday school. I packed the rest in my car and fled.

This Sunday school teacher in her yellow ski jacket had things to ponder. How often has some child seen me irritable and cross at the grocery store, impatient in line at the post office, hasty and insensitive at the cafeteria? We model good manners and cheerful acceptance at Sunday school, but what about on the town square? What about the nitty-gritty moments of truth in our lives? The truth is, once a teacher, always a teacher. We cannot escape the fact that the children see us always in that capacity, even when they are much older, and they will model their behavior on that of a beloved adult. Surely these three little girls had selected their new coats with the same care, and using the same mannerisms, that I had brought to bear on selecting that ski jacket.

It is only when we seek God's help that we can live up to the task of being a role model. The Bible is full of admonition for the one who teaches. It is very clear that we have grave responsibilities. When Paul speaks of the gifts of the spirit, teaching is high on this important list. Teaching in the church takes place in many ways besides formal instruction. Every disciple of Jesus Christ teaches by words and actions throughout his or her lifetime.

I was invited to lead a laboratory school in a church where I had once been a member. Children also attend this unique teacher-training event. One little fellow approached me saying, "Myrtle, did you know that you taught my daddy when he was a little boy?"

"Yes, I do," I agreed amiably.

"Huh," said another boy standing near. "That's nothing. She taught my Grandma."

We all had a good laugh as I acknowledged that, too.

Teaching is not just for today. It's for life. Somebody is sure to remember that you were once his daddy's teacher.

My Daddy Ain't a Jesus Man

We set a box of children's books bought at a yard sale in the Rap and Read area at the town hall, where we were holding vacation church school. Several children arrived early each day to read books and talk with the enabler in the center. There was no longer a church in this small town, but there were committed Christian adults who were eager to work with the children of the community.

I noticed that one child read the same book at least once each day, a colorful book with pictures of Jesus. We had told the children that at the end of the week, each child could choose a book to keep.

"Would you like to keep that book?" I asked her on the last day. She closed the book and laid it reluctantly back in the box.

"Oh, no," she said. "My Daddy ain't a Jesus man, and he would just tear it up."

Which leads us directly to a challenge that is by no means local. Many of the families in the geographical area of our parish were totally unchurched. Many others had only tenuous ties to a church, perhaps through their parents or grandparents. There were many unchurched children from families of both privilege and poverty.

One of our goals was "to provide for every child an ongoing relationship with a caring, Christian adult." We intended to do this by offering at least one hundred hours of supervised Christian education each year through Sunday schools, after-school programs, vacation church schools, day camping and Super Saturdays. Each teacher was charged with keeping in touch with the students, attending their public school programs when possible, helping to get them involved in scouting programs, sending birthday cards, and (most fun!) showing up at the playground during the summer just to touch base and play a game or two with the youngsters. We intended to remain a non-intrusive but Christian presence in the life of the parish children.

A highlight of my day was often to drive the parish van to Main Street of some little town and wait for the children to gather for a game or two on the cement slab. They always came when they saw that van. It was a symbol for them that someone cared. They didn't mind the apples, either.

Parents responded in different ways. Some children were refused permission to come to the church after school if they had misbehaved at home the previous week. Other parents offered us after-school treats, helped with recreation, assisted teachers, and came to church special events. We found ourselves in tune with the national trend, however: after-school programs win the hearts of children, but do not usually result in church membership for their families.

A Bishop questioned one of the teachers, "Don't you get discouraged when you work week after week with these youngsters, and only one family has joined the church?" Catherine answered, "No. If it weren't for this after-school ministry, some of these children would never have heard the name of Jesus."

The daddy who was not a Jesus man was not alone. A mentally disabled man, injured in an accident, was now unable to fathom the needs of his family or even to care. His children grew up like lost puppies.

A young girl in a small town gave birth to a child in her bed one dark night, and did not know what was happening.

Three children slept in a dusty rusted car in the yard. Their arms and legs were covered with weeping sores. I visited with their mother, who saw nothing unusual about the situation. The children did not appear at either Sunday school or vacation Bible school, and the family soon moved away.

There are endless such stories in areas of poverty. Teaching the unchurched children in Sunday school became more than a Sunday morning class or an after-school ministry. We needed to guide parents to sources of help, bring children to security, warmth and friendship, and win their trust before they could even begin to understand the Jesus stories we told them, or the assurance of God's love.

I wish I knew more about the little girl whose Daddy was not a Jesus man. This child, like so many others, moved with her family to another state.

I wish she had taken the book.

Visitors in the Night

There was an incessant banging on the door that morning. My husband checked the clock. 3:00 a.m. "Someone must have run out of gas," he grumbled as he pulled on his jeans and went to answer the door. Two frightened girls stood on the porch.

"Is Myrtle here?" I heard their scared voices, so I hurried out of bed. Two young girls from a nearby small town stood shivering on our doorstep.

Once inside and warmed up, they told me their story. I asked the girls to call their parents, who were probably worried sick, right away. They admitted that they were afraid to do so and hoped to sneak into their houses, if only I would drive them home.

These young girls, barely in their teens, had been "picked up" at the county seat by some boys from another county. When asked to go for a ride around the town square they consented, only to have their sense of adventure quickly turn into apprehension. The boys drove out of the county seat and started for another town. When the boys began making sexual references and advances, the girls resisted and begged to be allowed out of the car.

The boys obliged. They opened the doors, shoved the girls out in the middle of a dark winter night in open country, and promptly roared away. The only thing the girls could think of was that my house was on that highway. They turned east and began to walk. Frightened by approaching cars, they ran into the ditches to hide whenever they saw a car's lights. By the time they reached our house, it was 3:00 a.m., and these girls were cold and thoroughly chastened, dirty and covered with ditch trash. They were ready to promise me anything if only I would give them a ride home!

After the girls were warmed up and cleaned up, we talked about responsibility. I tried not to lecture (a great difficulty, I admit), but I asked the girls, "What would have been the responsible thing for the boys to do when you asked to get out of the car?" They agreed that the boys should have followed them until they reached safety, even if they would not re-enter the car.

My husband agreed to call the sheriff if I were not home in an hour. The girls and I set forth to confront parents.

What to do? I suggested that I go to the door in each case and explain to the parents. We came to an agreement. If lights were on in the houses, indicating that the parents were awake and worried, I would go to the door to try to deflect anger and judgment. If the houses were dark, I would simply wait until each one was safely inside her house and then drive away, making contact the next morning.

Both houses were dark. I couldn't believe it! Who had the parents expected to bring their daughters home from the county seat in the first place? Did they assume their daughters were staying all night with their girl friends? I did not know the parents personally at that time, only that they all were hard-working people with jobs. Could they possibly sleep that soundly when their daughters were not yet home?

I eased on home, where my own husband was not too happy about my going to the home of strangers in the early hours of the morning. When I contacted the girls the next day, both said that their parents did not realize that the whole thing had happened, and they weren't telling. Since I was their teacher and counselor of the youth group they attended, I told each of them that they were not off the hook. What changes in their behavior could I expect? Both girls promised me solemnly that she would not make any more misjudgments, especially about getting into a car with a strange boy.

Sometime later I visited one of these homes. We talked about the midnight visit. The mother shrugged the whole thing off. "It's part of growing up, I guess," she said.

Still, I kept tab of these girls. They continued to come to our nondenominational youth group, where my co-teacher and I tried really hard to teach morals, good judgment, and responsibility, as well as other Bible truths. In a couple years, one of the girls dropped out of high school and out of youth group. Later, her family moved out of town. The other girl graduated and moved on also.

Years later I was approached in a grocery store by a young woman who eagerly dug in her purse for her wallet of pictures. "Look!" she said. "Here is my older son, the one I had when I dropped out of school. He is a wonderful kid! Here is my husband and our other children. Here is my ID card as a nurse in a big hospital." When I had admired her whole family, their good grades in school, her handsome husband, her great career, she added one thing more.

"I never forgot that night along the road," she said, "or how scared we were. We thought you might throw us out of your house when you heard what we had done. I can't think why you trusted us. I made some mistakes in my life, but every time I remembered that I was responsible for myself and responsible to God."

I still see our Night Visitor now and then. She is a well-respected woman in her new town, successful in her career, with a great family. But I sometimes wonder: Did I do the right thing that night? Should I have aroused the parents, rather than taking upon myself the responsibility of being their mentor, of keeping an eye on these girls as nearly as I could? Would I have retained their confidence if I had reported the incident to their parents right away?

Since both girls attended the county seat high school, we had other contacts besides youth group. My co-teacher, a fine Christian man, also knew the families well and continued to relate to them at community gatherings, though neither of these families came to church.

But the question persists: How many kids can a person mentor and still do it effectively? And how responsible are we for each other?

Every day in our lives there are children and youth who make greater mistakes than these girls made. Possibly our communities need to take greater responsibility for guiding and guarding them.

There is something we can all do.

Be there for kids. Let them know you are there for them. Be on their side. When they are wrong, hold their feet to the fire. Keep tab. When they are right, acknowledge and praise them. When they make serious misjudgments, hold them responsible. None of us adults are paragons of virtue, and we never were. But we got to be adults by learning responsibility, by trusting someone, whether parents, teachers or mentors, to smooth the way by teaching values and insisting that they had the authority to do so. Some of us were fortunate enough to have Christian parents and mentors who gave religious nurture and guidance and helped us to know Jesus Christ.

No one will ever tell you that there is such a long list of duties and privileges for a Sunday school teacher. But if not you, who? In a time with so many modern "conveniences," it seems that people are busier than ever. Some parents spend less than ten minutes a day with their children. Mentoring programs, either formal or informal, can provide children with the support they need to grow into responsible individuals.

You may never know what the result will be as you mentor and teach a child. Vera and Heather came to a small country church for years. They waited at the door every Sunday for my husband and me to arrive. They insisted on sitting between us during worship. We had no children at the time and enjoyed Vera and Heather, urging them to attend Sunday school, where I was Vera's teacher.

I saw little of the girls after they moved. But years later I was sitting in a doctor's waiting room when I noticed a young woman looking curiously at me. When I met her glance repeatedly, she finally came to me to ask, "You are Myrtle, aren't you? I wanted to tell you that I married a Christian man and have a Christian home. I will never forget the teachers that Heather and I had at that little church when we were children. We learned to love Jesus there. Please thank the people at that church for us."

It is clear to me that what is known today as mentoring is included in the teaching role that Paul listed as among the gifts of the Spirit in the New Testament. As teachers, we thank God for our calling to be in Christian education and formation. As the friends and advocates of children, we hold the memory of each child warmly and prayerfully in our hearts.

A Place I've Never Been

Brad was a happy, outgoing boy who found something interesting about everyone he met. He conversed with adults as easily as with the boys his own age. Brad suffered rheumatic fever as a child, necessitating daily antibiotics until he was eighteen years old, but that never slowed Brad down. Gregarious, full of fun, keen about sports, an all-state football player and track star, Brad was the kind of kid you felt happy to be around.

Brad's family, his parents and brother Mike, were church members and leaders, and well-liked and respected in their community. Their warm, inviting home was a place where Brad, Mike, and their buddies liked to hang out. The boys attended Sunday school, after-school ministries, and youth group. They enjoyed the outdoors, especially their family fishing trips, and they were always eager to be on the move to see and experience new things. They were a closely bonded family, especially Brad and his brother Mike, who was just one year younger than Brad.

After high school, Brad chose a career in archeology. He earned a double major at Luther College of Iowa and found employment as an archeologist with the United States Forest Service in Medicine Bow National Forest in Wyoming.

There, Brad met a group of people of his own ilk, the Alpine Mountain Club. He began mountain climbing, conquering most of the Rocky Mountain peaks. Brad was ready to move on to high adventure! He wanted to go places where he had never been before. He and his friends journeyed to Argentina, where they climbed Mt. Aconcagus, at 22,835 feet, raising $22,835 for the Save the Children Federation. They bicycled across the entire continent of Australia, a ninety-day trip that covered 3,600 miles. Brad loved challenges, and he loved the outdoors.

But his biggest adventure was still ahead.

Brad and three friends embarked on a thirty-day "Ocean to Ice Cap Expedition" in 1995. One part of this Arctic adventure was to establish a new record, to traverse the Bathan Island Barnes Polar Ice Cap via bicycles. The four young people, now in their early thirties, were all good friends, adventurers who had climbed mountains, bicycled across wilderness areas, lovers of the great outdoors and eager to meet new challenges.

Equipped with special studded tires, the foursome made the successful summer trip across the ice cap, energized by the stunning scenery and their own sense of adventure. Truly, they were going where they had never been before!

Arriving back at the meeting point where their Eskimo guide was to meet them with a boat and the survival gear they had shipped ahead, the group had trouble establishing radio contact. Once established, they learned that their guide was on a fishing expedition and would not be available to get them for a few days. Disappointed but not particularly worried, the young friends pitched their tents on a beautiful beach and inventoried their remaining food. They had enough for two days. They could do this.

Somewhat grungy after two weeks without a shower, but still excited and pleased with their accomplishment, the friends built a campfire, enjoyed a hot drink, and carefully rationed out a day's food. With a pencil Brad wrote in his journal that he did not seem particularly upset about the guide's failing to show up. Perhaps they themselves had arrived earlier than expected. Still, the shortage of food was worrisome. At most, they would have three hundred calories a day each, not nearly enough for the active bodies of these young people. After an evening of sharing around the campfire, they rolled into their sleeping bags. Maybe tomorrow they would be off the beach and headed for home.

The next few days brought anxiety to the group. When they were able to make minimum contact through the radio, they learned that the guide would not be able to arrive for another few days. They were firm in their statements that they needed to be picked up immediately. They were out of food. Apparently trying to be helpful, their contact told them not to be alarmed, "there is food all around you."

By this undoubtedly the Eskimo people of the village meant the berries that did seem plentiful. The friends began to search for likely looking leaves, which they combined with native berries and a third of a package of instant chicken soup found in a backpack. Each one had a third of a cup of this delicious stew, according to Brad's journal. They were so energized they immediately began collecting more leaves!

Another time they found blueberries. What a feast! After fresh blueberries and a good helping of fried native berries, Brad's stomach didn't feel nearly so hollow, but he recorded that their situation was becoming critical. Again they were able to establish tentative radio contact, during which they were told that the boat was broken down. The guide would come as soon as he could.

By now lethargy had set in for these calorie-starved adventurers. The last half-cup of chocolate was gone. Most of their energy was spent searching for berries and huddling in their sleeping bags or around the fire trying to keep warm. Water temperatures, even in the Arctic summer, were frigid. Scenes of the awesome mountains, cliffs and fjords they had experienced provided them with hours of conversation.

At last a sturdy eighteen-foot boat piloted by a single Eskimo guide arrived with plenty of food. Tents and supplies were hauled aboard, and an enthusiastic group, stomachs well filled, headed back to their base camp. Only the slightest worry must have tugged at their minds. The survival gear they had shipped ahead had not arrived. They still wore their Arctic hiking togs, while only the guide wore survival gear.

As they headed back to their base camp, they spotted a pod of bowhead whales frolicking in the cold waters. Bowheads are large animals, considered docile and even playful. The young adventurers decided to move in closer to the pod in order to take pictures.

It was at this point that the Eskimo guide noticed a whale approaching the boat. The animal swam under the boat, overturning it and casting the five into the frigid arctic water. The water temperature was about thirty-six degrees.

The group was immediately aware of the life threatening danger. Hypothermia deaths resulting from such cold water are not uncommon in the Arctic. People wearing normal water gear perish in these waters as quickly as thirty minutes. Those in survival gear may live much longer. Among the five, only the guide wore survival gear.

Alone in the ocean, far from shore or from any other source of help, Brad and his friends knew that it was only a matter of time before they would all perish.

Although they tried valiantly to set the boat upright, it was an impossible task. In the end, they climbed on the upside-down boat, one at a time, for rest periods. The others clung to the sides of the overturned boat until, one by one, they slipped into the water. Only the guide, in survival gear, survived the hours of agony until rescued by a search boat.

Few of their possessions were recovered, though thankfully Brad's journal survived and can be read since it was written in pencil. The guide recounted to Brad's parents those last terrible hours in the water.

"They never complained," he said. "They prayed and sang hymns and held on as long as they could. Just before Brad let go, he said, 'Please tell my family thanks for everything they have done for me. Tell them I love them. Tell them I am okay, that I've made my peace with God, and I'm going someplace I have never been before." Shortly after this, Brad slipped from the side of the boat and was lost beneath the arctic waters.

The guide clung to the boat, the only survivor. As the last young man gave in to the waters, the guide saw a white, translucent cloud rise from the waters and ascend above the boat. The guide felt the presence of an overwhelming power and felt certain that the souls of the four young adventurers were ascending to God. He told Brad's parents that he gained the strength from this miracle to hold on for many more hours. Each time he was ready to give up and let go, he heard a voice saying, "Be strong." At last he was picked up by a rescue boat and taken to his village. From there he called the parents of each of his young friends who had so courageously faced death.

John, Linda, and Mike Humphrey treasure Brad's journal and the memory of this very special young man. Today, Mike is married. He and his wife have given John and Linda two wonderful, happy grandchildren. The family speaks often of Brad, glad to share the story of this adventurous free spirit with interested and loving friends. They take comfort and assurance in the guide's account of the event, knowing that Brad is safe with God in a place that he has never been before.

"We want his story to do some good," says John. "Brad loved the earth and all its wonders, and he knew in his final moments that he was going on yet another adventure. We believe in the miracle of his soul going to God at the moment of death."

Nurturing children in faith in Jesus Christ is the most important thing any of us will ever do. Most of us will never experience the loss of John and Linda, but all of us can take comfort when we have provided the nurturing homes and church communities that give strength and meaning to the lives of young people.

His school, his community and his church remember Brad. He makes us dream of places where we, too, have never been.

And we know that when we arrive where Brad is, we will find him climbing new mountains of faith and joy in the presence of God.

Under the Bridge

It happened in a small town in Iowa. Back in the late 70s, there was not much to do in a little burg of around two hundred members. There were no busses, taxis, or trains out of town. Kids fished and swam in a nearby pond, played at a town playground, and tossed balls around in a vacant lot. Everyone knew everyone else, and some attended one of the two churches in town. Still, there were a lot of unchurched kids. We organized a youth group—everyone welcome, refreshments served. It's not hard to get a group of youth together under those circumstances.

Almost everyone in the group dealt with a problem of one kind or another. One girl needed eye surgery. Several lived in single-parent homes. There was a boy with a physical challenge. We got along, had fun together, studied our Bible lessons, prayed for each other, and ate a lot of pizza. The good ladies of the church where we met (no men in the congregation at the time) kept the rooms spotlessly clean, did not mind if we used the kitchen, and encouraged whatever parties or projects we had in mind. It was pretty neat.

Only one evening, there was no way anyone could concentrate. The boys were bickering and using strong language, and the girls were taking sides. I insisted on knowing the cause of our trouble.

It seemed that one boy had a disagreement with another. He had then gone under a nearby bridge and painted some nasty graffiti about the other boys. I called a halt to the arguments. We worked our way through a long consultive process and decided that the only way to proceed with reconciliation was to remove the writing from under the bridge.

We agreed to meet the next week at the church. The boy who had written the words was to get permission from the Board of Supervisors to paint underneath the bridge. We would all ride the parish fifteen passenger van to the site, bringing cans of spray paint.

Good plan. All went according to schedule. I let the kids out at the bridge, and then drove a short way to the nearest driveway to turn around, heading the van back to the church. I parked along the road and walked to the ditch. There I was met by two of the students.

"Please don't go under the bridge," they said. "Just wait here until we are finished painting."

"No," I objected. "We agreed that we would do this together. I am part of the group, too. I intend to go under the bridge."

"Myrtle," said one with that infinite patience one reserves for a three-year-old, "you can't. We *voted*."

All right. I, who had taught these kids about democracy, fair play, majority rule, and responsibility, had now been voted out of the group. I sat on the grass and tried to figure out what to do next, while peals of laughter rolled up from under the bridge. Would red and green and purple kids soon emerge?

No such luck. We piled into the van and returned to the church. Everyone agreed that writing under the bridge had been a dumb thing to do, but it was now forgiven and the words blotted out for future generations. I never went under the bridge and haven't to this day. After all, the kids voted.

What did I learn about teaching? I learned that sometimes you have to lay aside that carefully crafted Bible lesson and deal with the life issue at hand. I felt convinced that "Forget about it and move on" may sometimes work, but at other times it leaves a residue of ill feeling and resentment. Dealing upfront with the original problem, removing words written in the heat of passion, figuring out a way for them to deal with their own feelings, and asking for God's direction in our lives, made reconciliation real and lasting. We worked hard at getting along.

Being voted out of the group? I learned that kids sometimes want to protect teachers, too, and they really didn't want me to know they could use such foul language. Or perhaps they even thought all those words would be new to me!

A really bad winter followed this escapade. Snow was piled high all over this little town. Oddly enough, I noticed one day that a few foot prints led to the crawl space at the back of the church building. I went to investigate, thinking this was not a very safe place for children to be playing, but I found nothing—just tracks leading both in and out of the crawl space.

I mentioned it to the youth group and drew some comment. There was a homeless youth in town. His parents had moved away, leaving him with a relative until the end of the school year. When the relative thought the boy was uncontrollable, she simply told him to leave. So he lived wherever a friend would put him up for a night. One night none of his friends was available, and he slept in the crawl space under the church. I asked where he ate, and the kids told me that sometimes he showed up at their houses at mealtime and would be invited to share. Other times the kids just brought him food from home and gave it to him on the school bus.

Small towns and rural areas deal with poverty, homelessness, drop-outs, drugs and alcohol just as much as the cities do, only frequently it is less visible. Recent surveys show that millions of children live in poverty in America alone. Many are disenfranchised, marginalized by poverty and family conditions over which they have no control. One in seven rural Americans is poor. Most of these are women and children.

Eventually, the crawl-space youth graduated and rejoined his parents in another state. Other youth in this small town continued to deal in various ways with their problems.

Some of these kids received camp scholarships from a generous man in our community, who gave his income tax refund for that purpose. When I picked up the kids at camp in the parish van, one boy had an exciting tale of service to tell.

"We were all hungry the first day or two," he said. "They didn't budget enough money to give us all we wanted to eat. So I told the camp director to let me help shop, because I knew how. So I went with them to shop for groceries, and then we all had enough."

I could only imagine that they ate a lot of potatoes and mac and cheese. But I was proud of this fellow, and he was proud of himself. Camp greatly increased his self-awareness and self-confidence. This teenager also told me, "I didn't know there were so many nice people. Everyone treated me good." Duane began to attend church worship services and soon assumed a leadership role among the high schoolers.

Several years later a young man rang my doorbell. He said, "You don't know me, do you, Myrtle? I just stopped in to say hello." This successful young man, who obviously still knew how to plan and shop, told me about his life and his hopes over a cup of coffee.

Duane's camp and youth group experiences had changed his life.

We Sunday school teachers deny ourselves a great privilege if we do not seek to serve and teach the forgotten children and youth of our community. It is through the presence of the Holy Spirit that we are able to develop a gift for teaching, and to experience deep happiness and joy from the art of teaching. It is not always easy, and solutions to problems are not always evident. But God, who gives the gift of teaching, will also give the gift of wisdom if we are persistent and faithful.

Please Call the Hospital

A message like this sends your heart to your heels. Is your spouse ill? Has your child been in an accident? Is this a community or terrorist emergency?

Marlene was an only child. Her parents were hard working people with good jobs. Though they did not have other relatives in Iowa, they had good neighbors who enjoyed Marlene and invited her to Sunday school. Marlene's parents did not come to church, but Marlene enjoyed being there and soon began coming to the Wednesday after-school program as well. She was a likeable child; her neighbors, who were grandparents several times over, encouraged Marlene in her school and church activities. This is the neighbor who asked me to call the hospital.

Marlene's father, who had not seemed particularly depressed to his acquaintances, had committed suicide. During the night he started his car, which was in an attached garage, left a suicide note, and died of carbon monoxide poisoning. Tragically, the carbon monoxide had seeped into the house. Marlene's mother in the bedroom above the garage also died. Marlene was in very serious condition and was being flown by helicopter to the university hospital.

I called the nurses every morning for a report on Marlene. At last I was told that visitors were now welcome. I drove to the hospital and was terribly saddened to see a totally inert child, not at all the lively, talkative girl we had known. An aunt from Texas was making arrangements to come to Iowa for an extended period with her niece. In the meantime, the nurses felt that any familiar object from Marlene's home might help her to regain awareness of her surroundings and stimulate brain activity. I promised to do what I could.

Thank God for small towns! The city police agreed to come with me to the home to retrieve any toy or familiar object that might help Marlene. I don't remember if we got a court order or if a neighbor simply had a key. At any rate, a police officer and I went to the home and found some stuffed toys in Marlene's bedroom. The police made a careful list of what we removed, and I started the long trip back to the hospital. The nurses lay a stuffed toy in Marlene's arms. The rest we perched on shelves and chairs. There was absolutely no reaction from Marlene.

During the difficult weeks that followed, I spoke often with Marlene's aunt. She expressed gratefulness to the neighbor who had seen that Marlene got to Sunday school, and to the church that cared for Marlene through many weeks of convalescence. This marvelous woman had put her own life aside to help in her niece's recovery.

Although Marlene recovered slowly, she was finally able to travel. She returned to Texas with her aunt to resume her life with her cousins in that family. She never returned to the home where the tragedy occurred. Although her speech and mobility were seriously affected, Marlene was able to return to school.

The whole church teaches. Christian education happens in many ways aside from formal instruction in the Bible, important as that is. We think of the caring, supportive love of Marlene's Christian neighbor, of the stacks of cards and gifts Marlene received from her friends in Sunday school and Wednesday school, of the prayers of her pastors and the whole congregation, of the caring police department. We all learned that we are never alone, that Jesus loves each of us. "We love, because he first loved us" is not just a song to our children, it is an experience. Thank God!

That same call came another day, just as I was departing on a trip. "Please come to the hospital." When I arrived, a small child was about to undergo an appendectomy. She had suffered terrible stomach pains in the night. A neighbor finally convinced the parents to take her to the hospital, where they signed a number of papers and left.

My phone calls to members of our congregation were not frantic, but they were certainly urgent. "We have a little girl who needs a loving grandmother for at least a week. She is in surgery now, so you could probably count on being at the hospital all night. She will need much support in the days ahead."

One of the things I have learned as a Sunday school teacher is not to pull punches when I need help. The more urgent and difficult the task, the more readily one can find help! People simply do not like to do volunteer, busy-work tasks. Boomers especially want their volunteer tasks to be meaningful and worthwhile.

Not only did we find a grandmother for Susan, grandpa came, too. They stayed vigilantly beside her all night, bought her a radio, and new clothes to wear home. Her parents finally came to check on her and took her home.

Few knew that at home Susan had no bed. She slept on a pile of old clothes in one corner of the kitchen. When her temporary grandfather discovered this, he bought Susan her first bed. Shortly thereafter, the whole family moved away, Susan, bed, and all. We never heard from them again.

Susan's temporary grandparents never forgot her. They became active as child advocates, raising the awareness of the church community of the problems and challenges faced by some of our children. Most of these people were astonished to know that children lived in such poverty and neglect in our rich and fertile state. Others denied it, saying, "If they would get a better job, they wouldn't have to live off the rest of us."

God moved mightily among us as we sought to be more inclusive, caring Christians.

It was at this point that we realized that we needed trained people ready to mentor and guide children and their families, Christians who wanted to express their faith through action. This was not universal by any means! There were those who complained that the doorknobs of the restrooms were always dirty when the after-school children met at church. The custodian and I considered washing doorknobs to be a ministry and had a lot of laughs as we polished up those doorknobs each week! Others complained that it was all just play, no Bible to it. We began a program whereby those who provided kitchen help would take twenty minutes before the children arrived to visit the learning centers, thereby experiencing how we were teaching about Jesus Christ. Retired people came in to help children with woodworking, gift making, and field trips.

High school and junior high youth who wanted to help with the children at vacation church school, Sunday school, or after-school ministries had their own group called Young Christian Educators. We met on Saturday mornings, dividing our time into Bible study, teaching methods, and pizza eating. Well, maybe some games and tall tales, too!

Because people were trained for the task, had confidence they could do it well, and were appreciated by the faith community, there was never a time when a Sunday school teacher could not find the help he or she needed. The needs were not usually so dramatic as the calls for Susan and Marlene, but we were learning the needs of our community and how to respond as followers of Jesus.

Which leads me to reflect that teachers learn as much from the teaching experience as the students do.

Sometimes that learning constitutes knowing the Bible better, which is a form of informational learning. Other times we learn how to apply the Bible better to our own lives, and we teach the youngsters to apply the teachings of Jesus to their lives. We call that formational learning. Together we are informed and formed, daily becoming more like the people that Jesus wants us to be. As we respond to the needs of our communities, how grateful we are for the saving power of Jesus, and for the constant guidance of the Holy Spirit!

The Lesson

I met my friend David the summer that the street past the church was being repaved. Great gouges were made as pipes were exposed, old cement was hauled away, a new roadbed was prepared. Then the rains came and the street was deep in mud and clay. It was weeks before we could use Washington Street.

Fortunately, our church was on a corner, so with a few changes in my route, I could drive to the church. Every morning I was greeted by a cheery voice calling across Washington Street. David was ten years old, he told me, and had just moved to town. He didn't know any kids yet. He enjoyed playing along the street, and one day he brought his skateboard to show me. I admired it, telling him that there weren't any skateboards when I was a kid, but I enjoyed seeing him ride on the sidewalk on his side of the street. For several days we discussed skateboards, roller skates, basketballs, and school. He was getting to know a few kids in the neighborhood.

One morning when I arrived, David was waiting to greet me…on my side of the street…with two skateboards. I laid my books under a bush as David carefully issued his instructions. He held my hand as I stepped onto the skateboard. Even though I was forced to jump off rather quickly, David was quietly encouraging.

"You can do this," he said. "You said you used to roller skate. The balance is different, but you can catch on." David encouraged, gave generous hints on technique, made sure he was near in case I started to take a bad fall. We practiced until I could go across three cracks in the sidewalk. Then David concluded my lesson, picked up his skateboards and went home, a very circuitous route that enabled him to get across Washington Street.

I had a lesson almost every day for a while. David and I rolled along the sidewalk in front of the church, taking mutual pleasure in our companionship. As he began to meet more kids on his side of the street, the frequency of the lessons diminished, but we still called good morning across Washington Street and had an occasional skate together. David showed me all the possibilities that were ahead of me with a skateboard, even though I seldom traveled more than three cracks at a time.

Summer moved on. Vacation Bible schools and day camps ate up the weeks, and I did not see David quite as often. Then one morning when I arrived at the church, David was sitting on the front steps.

"I have to move away," he said solemnly. "My dad has a better job. I came to say good-bye." David handed me the loveliest large red tomato I ever saw. "It's from our garden," he said. "It's the best one. We want you to have it."

I never taught David in Sunday school since he and his parents were members of another denomination. Our relationship was totally centered around skateboards and morning conversations across Washington Street. But David taught me more than just skateboarding.

a. When you move to a new place, contact people and make friends. Don't let a muddy street stop you. Use your outdoor voice.

b. If another person doesn't have a skateboard, offer to share.

c. When you're teaching someone how to do something, explain it first. Then show them how you do it. Then help.

d. Be patient with people who are afraid and maybe clumsy or maybe older. With a little practice they might get it. Be encouraging. Tell them it is great if they can go across three cracks in the sidewalk without falling off their skateboards.

e. Tell people you have faith in them. Sometimes they must do things they never thought they could do. Say, "You can do it. I know you can do it."

f. Stick by your friends. Don't worry if it takes a little extra time.

g. Go out of your way to make a difference. You can easily walk a few extra blocks if you think it is important.

h. If you have to leave someone, say good-bye and give him or her your best tomato.

That wisdom has stood me in good stead for a long time.

The Peanut Butter Boy

Jimmy was a fun boy, the oldest of several brothers who lived with their parents in a former tavern on Main Street. The downstairs served as living room and kitchen. The upstairs, with its own steps on the outside of the building, had once been a separate apartment, but now these rooms were bedrooms for a large family. These boys regularly attended an after-school program. The school was just across the street from the church, so we usually experienced a rush of kids to the church when the last school bell rang and the busses lined up for the country children.

Jimmy always tried to be one of the first in line for the sandwiches. The end of a school day almost demands a snack, and a few ladies of the church never failed to have plenty on hand. One day Jimmy said, "Oh, Helen, you make the best peanut butter sandwiches!"

"You must like peanut butter," Helen smiled.

"Oh, yes. Sometimes at night, when everybody is asleep, I sneak downstairs and open my daddy's jar and smell it."

It wasn't that Jimmy never got peanut butter. It's just that his daddy was a working man who took his lunch box to work, and there had to be something to put in it. Sneaking peanut butter was forbidden. But even a smell was worth a trip down those dark outside steps.

Helen never forgot Jimmy's remark, and she never failed to have a jar of peanut butter. Since her home was right next to the church, children often came to Helen's porch to see her dog or to wait for the school bus out of the rain. One morning Helen noticed some noses pressed to her screen door right after breakfast.

"Would you like some toast?" she asked two little girls. As she was preparing their toast, Helen noticed that one little girl was licking her finger, then pressing it on the crumbs that were on the table and hastily licking them off her finger. This child was hungry. Since there was no breakfast program at the school, Helen could only surmise that this little girl would normally have to wait for the school lunch before she ate that day.

Summer Bible school ministries ran into the same situation. Children arrived at the town center for Bible school whenever they awakened, mostly without breakfast. The mission group that sponsored Bible school began bringing breakfast. Volunteers from fifty miles away would arrive with fruit and toast for hungry children.

Unusual? We wish. We are told that one out of every seven rural persons lives in poverty. One third of those become "food insecure" sometime during the year. Again, the majority of the poor in America are women and children.

David Beckmann, president of Bread for the World, indicates that rural communities, whether in America or around the world, have one thing in common. Rural people are more likely to be hungry and poor than any other citizens of their country. ("One in seven rural Americans is poor," May 3, 2005, *Christian Century*.) Here in the middle of America's breadbasket, there are undernourished children.

There are farmers raising cattle on the green hills of our county who do well, and there is industry in the county seat. Most of the small towns, however, have much unemployment or underemployment. Once these were thriving coalmining towns, but both population and opportunity decreased when the coalmines began to close in the 50s. Many of these citizens moved to cities in other states to find employment. Those who remained did so for reasons of family, lack of education, or simply because they love the green land. The coalmines are completely gone, but problems of poverty and lack of job opportunity remain.

I have seen earthen floors where children live. I have seen unwashed children with phlegm and feces all over their bodies. I have seen the little girl who did not have water in the house to wash her hair, so she used the coffee on the stove before going to school. I have talked with kindly public school teachers who have sent children to the gym showers for a clean up before class. I have coaxed grocery stores and bakeries for their day-old rolls and doughnuts to give children snacks after school. People from all over our conference have sent money to help buy the peanut butter that Jimmy and his friends loved.

These are only band-aides for hunger. School breakfasts and lunches now assure that our children receive basic nutrition. Sometimes families appeal to the ministerial assocations for help, but they are given limited trips a month to this emergency supply. Some churches keep their own shelves of basics.

It is hard to teach a child whose stomach is growling, whose head might be itchy. Teachers often give up, even Sunday school teachers, and no longer invite or tend these children. One of the brightest boys I know came from this kind of small town. His advantage was a grandmother who cared about him and was able to help him out of the situation. He is now an intelligent, educated young man with a job, a future, and a church where he is respected and loved.

We cannot give up on any youngster. The poor and hungry are the invisible children of many communities. A small mentally handicapped boy sat on the stoop of his home for years, shaking a rag. He had no one to play with, no one to oversee his development. The adult in his household would not answer the door when I called. So he shook his rag, all alone there on the stoop, and had only a gargle to greet me as I sat beside him for a moment.

Another child of a racially mixed family had such severe mental and behavioral problems that his parents kept him in a dog pen under a tree during the day in the summertime. One of the problems with securing community care for such children results partly from joblessness. When a Human Resources person visits, within days some of these families are gone from the community, taking their children and their problems with them. There is seldom a job to hold them to an area of poverty.

Please look for the invisible children. They are there. They are children of God. We must bring the love and care of

Jesus Christ to bear on the problems of these children of the poor.

Don't forget to bring plenty of peanut butter.

She Ain't Heavy

What a great kid Larry was! When he first began bringing his sister to Sunday school, he was in about fourth grade. Beth was a first grader, and Larry watched over her like a hawk.

He would not attend his own class, but prevailed upon us to let him remain in first grade with Beth. I made him my helper, and he really was a good addition to our younger elementary class.

Larry, however, was one of those kids who was always bullied. His family was very poor. His father did not work, having been seriously injured in a hunting accident. Besides, he had an uncertain reputation in his community. They lived in substandard housing. Perhaps the bullying was mostly because of his family background, but Larry would take any kind of insult to protect Beth. Never had a little girl a more determined warrior!

One day, when Larry left the church, some bigger neighborhood bullies attacked him. When they threw bricks at him, he retreated with a bloody nose to the church. We cleaned him up and got in the parish van, driving to his house to talk with his parents. Larry led me into the house where his father sat before a television set. He absolutely paid no attention to my words. Perhaps he was unable to do so. He kept his eyes on the TV and never turned his head in our direction.

As I turned to leave, Larry's mother came home carrying two jugs of milk. With one swoop of her arm, Ma Kettle fashion, she cleared enough space on the table to set them down.

"Larry has been hurt," I said. "I don't think his nose is broken, but I would be glad to take him to the hospital if you wish." She exploded in a storm of expletives. She simply couldn't understand why the bigger boys always picked on her kid.

When it was obvious that she had other concerns and did not want her son seen in the emergency room, I said goodbye to Larry and Beth and left.

Another time Larry swallowed a pin. Again, I took him home. I explained to his mother (Dad was still in front of the TV) that the church had insurance, and if she wanted I would take him for an x-ray. That didn't help a thing; she refused to be concerned.

"It'll pass," she shrugged. Apparently this was not the first object Larry had swallowed.

Eventually this family fared better in life and moved to a larger and neater home. Larry still protected Beth. They had another brother and a sister, but one usually saw just Larry and Beth together. The two of them moved quietly through town, trying to avoid trouble, to be invisible and insignificant at school, and to attending Sunday school and after-school ministries, where they enjoyed the snacks and the stories.

However, their troubles were not over. Fire of unknown cause destroyed their home. Several lives were lost, among them Beth. Larry was devastated. He had not been able to save Beth, nor either of his parents.

Every child has something to teach us. Larry had a rough row to hoe. His own experience as a target for bullying made him determined to protect his little sister. Perpetually pale and thin, he guarded that little girl on the playground, on the streets, in church, and probably at home. He was a vigilant and protective child, scarcely older than the sibling he protected. Undoubtedly, this was at the sacrifice of many of his own desires. He did parental duty at the age of nine.

It was plain to see that Larry needed to be just a boy once in a while. At day camp, where he felt assured of Beth's interest and safety in her own group, he finally played ball with the other kids, enjoyed crafts, and got pretty good at both. One of our pastors took him fishing. We tried to open doors for him, to expand his interest, and relieve him somewhat of the task he had set for himself. Most of all we tried to give him hope for the future.

But courage, integrity, and selfless service to others, faithfulness—those we did not need to teach Larry. He showed all of us how to do it right.

Larry's brother tells me that Larry now lives in a large city, where he works at a battery factory. He has a good salary and benefits. His brother did not know if Larry belongs to a church. He is married. He and his wife have a daughter.

They named her Beth.

The Girl Who Wouldn't Talk

A distraught grandmother called me. Although I knew her slightly, I did not know that she was the grandmother of a child who came to an after-school program for elementary children in their small town. This child had many friends, and was a humorous and somewhat mischievous little girl. My first thought was that Amy had been in an accident.

I also did not know that her father was the man in the local newspaper headlines. He had committed suicide in his home, in the presence of his wife and children. The grandmother pleaded for me to come to her house, where the children were temporarily staying.

"Amy will not talk," she said. "It has been several days, and she hasn't spoken a word. She won't talk to her mother, her teacher, or even to her brother and sister." I asked if the school had referred her to our local mental health agency, where all kinds of help was available. I assured her that I had no training in psychology, but I would be glad to come to see her granddaughter, just to express my love and sympathy.

Once at her home, Grandmother and I spoke for several minutes. Amy solemnly watched us, eyes absolutely blank, saying nothing at all. Finally, I asked if I might take Amy to the park to play on the swings for a while. Amy nodded that she would like to go.

I opened the passenger door of the car for Amy, saw that she was buckled in properly, and walked around to the driver's side. I slid behind the wheel but had not even closed the car door before Amy began to talk.

"My dad and mom had a fight, and my dad said he was so mad he could shoot himself and my mom went and got the gun and he did."

Shock. Total shock.

I drove carefully to the park where we joined other girls and boys in swinging, going down the slide, and climbing on the jungle gym. Amy participated in all these activities, saying not a word.

An hour later we returned to her grandmother's home.

"You won't tell, Myrtle, will you? You won't tell?" pleaded Amy.

I agreed that I would not tell. However, I urged her to tell her grandmother, and I advised the grandmother to be sure to seek help immediately for Amy.

A week later Amy's grandmother called again. Amy's mother had taken her children and moved to Alaska, where she had relatives.

Although I realize that my feelings have absolutely nothing to do with this, I must admit that I was totally frustrated. Both school and church had advised seeking help for this traumatized little girl, yet she was totally removed from the sources of help, taken far from her normal surroundings, possibly out of fear that sooner or later she would talk about the circumstances of this tragedy. We can only pray that in Alaska her relatives saw the need and were able to help Amy.

It is so important for Sunday school teachers to strengthen their bonds with each student. But when something so overwhelming happens, about which we can do very little, we are apt to get discouraged.

Thankfully, we rejoice that we can love because God first loved us. We will not always know how a child turns out, or if the person is growing in faith and feels the presence of Jesus Christ in his or her life. Our goal should be to secure professional help for people who come to us if that seems necessary, and to love and tend them regardless. Jesus would do so, and we are his disciples.

A woman came to my home office not long ago. She just wanted to talk. When she began to share serious problems in her home situation, I advised her that I was not a counselor and offered to take her to our pastor. She sprang from her chair and angrily paced the floor.

"No!" she exclaimed. "I won't talk to a man! I won't talk to any man! I don't care if he is a pastor, I don't trust any man!" We continue to talk now and then, and to pray about her problems. Neither of us violates our trust relationship. We must trust the Holy Spirit to work good in our lives when we put our lives in the hand of God.

One day my pastor knocked at my door accompanied by a man who he introduced as Harry Denman. My pastor did not reveal that this was the Harry Denman known throughout the world for his humble demeanor, his willingness to take off his jacket and give it to the needy man he saw on the street, and his utter faithfulness to his Lord.

I had read about Harry Denman the evangelist, how his cheery words to a stranger in an office building elevator were usually, "Good morning! Do you know my friend Jesus?" As we visited that evening, I kept wondering if this was the same Harry Denman. Finally, I asked him.

"Mr. Denman, are you the Harry Denman from Nashville, who converts people in the elevator?"

"Oh, no!" he replied with a chuckle. There was a long pause. Then he said, "The Holy Spirit does that."

We teachers need to remember that our calling is to teach, to love, to help, to encourage, to understand, and even just to talk. We need to remember that work of conversion to Christ is the work of the Holy Spirit. It does not belong to us. We pray God's holiest blessing upon our teaching, and then we keep on keeping on.

Is Your Mother Home?

Home visitation can be either dreadful or delightful. I have encountered some of each.

One day I called at a home after school. This family had seven or eight children; I've forgotten how many. Our parish had some camp scholarship money, and I needed to talk with the parents about the possibility of two or three of their children going to camp.

The mother greeted me cheerfully and hurried to heat up the coffee. Later, sipping our coffee in the front room, I asked the age and grade in school of each child. We got off to a good start, but the further down the line we got, the more confused this mother became. She began to laugh because she couldn't get all those children straight, and I laughed with her.

In the middle of this merriment, the father came home from work. He put his lunch box on the counter, poured himself the rest of the coffee, then came into the living room to kiss his wife hello. He hugged all the children, including the baby. Then he went to the cage hanging by a window where a hamster was running wildly on his wheel. He opened the cage door, allowing the hamster to run up one arm, across his shoulders, down the other arm and back into the cage. He then collected a couple of the younger children and went outside to pet his dog and his goat. Outside he also found and hugged his two older boys.

All this time he was sipping coffee, sharing the news of the day with his wife and me, patting children on the head, dodging toys on the floor and, I hope, counting his kids. He was not a man in a hurry, and his wife finally was able to name all her children. I went home chuckling. A delightful call like this could set me up for a whole week.

But there were the other kind of visits, too. Right before Vacation Bible school I knocked on the door of a home where I had been told two children lived. A young boy invited me in, but when he indicated that his mother was not home, I said we could talk on the porch if that was okay with him.

About that time a woman came storming up the street and up the porch steps.

"What are you doing here?" she demanded. "Who are you?"

"I live on a farm just over that way," I said. I gave my name and stated my business. She was having none of it. "I don't want people here when I'm not home," she said. "I work at the tavern, but I can see my house. I don't want anyone around my house."

I left a flyer with the information, said good-bye to the boy, and hastened away.

I was never, never afraid when making house calls. I went prayerfully to each home, and if I was treated rudely I did not enter the house. Sometimes those children turned up later at a Parish Fun Day or a ballgame, and we could then issue an invitation to the child or to the whole family, warmly welcoming them to our worship and Sunday school.

During vacation Bible school in one of our small towns, we had visitors from our Conference office. They were interested in our Christian education outreach and had come to experience the community, visit in the homes, and talk with people. I directed them to several homes in the area. One was the home of a well-known cattle breeder, who had a lovely farmstead and was an active leader in the community. His several children were in vacation Bible school. I also directed them to a home within two miles of that lovely farm. These folks lived in a hut crowded with junk and broken down furniture. The children were also in vacation Bible school, and our visitors were able to talk with both sets of parents and children.

Our visitors went away in awe. It was clear that these neighbors were able to find common ground, wanted the best for their children, and worshipped side-by-side. Without the home visits, I doubt our guests could have appreciated that fact.

One memorable morning, three pastors and I visited every home in a small town. We invited Sunday school children to go with us. We divided the town into quadrants and took the children to make a pitch for vacation Bible school. What fun we had! The children seemed to know everyone in town and were not shy about introducing us. We pinned homemade buttons on each child that said, "VBS Missionary." By prearrangement, one church member gave us hot dogs and chips for lunch. We celebrated our largest vacation Bible school that year.

Sometimes, regretfully, things did not turn out so well. I had been asked to call on a woman who lived alone. Her friends thought she had been ill and would enjoy a call and a visit about Sunday school.

I knocked on the outside door of an enclosed porch, but there was no answer. A little hesitant, but still feeling it was okay, I entered the tiny porch and knocked on the door of the house. Still there was no answer. Thinking she was not home, I drove away and forgot the call for a few days.

I felt pleased when a letter arrived with this woman's return address, though I was not pleased for long! The letter revealed that she was upset that I had come onto her enclosed porch. She referred to my "trespassing," said she had weapons, and that if I drove into her yard again, she would use them. When I shared the letter with the friend who had asked me to call, she was as mystified as I was. After much thought and prayer, she was persuaded that this friend was on some medication that caused her change in personality. She got in touch with her friend's doctor, related the incident to him, and he cautiously said he would look into it.

I realized, of course, that I should have phoned this lady first before going to her home. Later on, she did come to worship a few times, and we greeted each other. I do not believe she even remembered writing the letter. After this experience, I began to follow my calling guides a little more respectfully.

a) Phone first, if at all possible. Give a brief reason for the call. "I heard you were ill and wanted to check if it would be okay to drop in to see you." "The girls have not been in Sunday school for two weeks. May I stop by with their take-home papers?" "We have a new class at Sunday school, and I would like to tell Jimmy about it. May I come after school?"

b) Always bring something—Not candy, not a bribe, but either an attractive brochure or an activity paper that children would enjoy doing. If you are not sure of the age level, bring a variety and let the children choose what they would like.

c) Arrive promptly when you say you will. Leave promptly. Folks have things to do, and they are generous to let you come in the first place.

d) If they offer a glass of lemonade or a piece of cake, enjoy it. They would not offer this ritual of eating together if they were not interested in what you have to say. Of course, if you are diabetic or have other allergies or health problems, explain those and ask for a glass of water. The important thing is to sit down. Their offer means something. Yes, there are homes where you will want to accept only coffee or water. Do it graciously. Remember, you are here because God loves these folks.

e) State your invitation or concern briefly, but cordially. Talk with the children. If you do not know them well, ask about their school, their hobbies, their pets. Ask the adults if they have any questions. Be open to the possibility that they might want to talk about something else, now that they have you there. When you leave, say, "God bless you!"

f) Follow up with a small note. "I enjoyed our visit. Thank you for the coffee and for the time together. I hope to see you in Sunday school soon."

g) If you feel uncomfortable or threatened in any way, do not enter the house. If you are already there, casually mention, "You are one of the families I told my pastor (husband, whatever) I would visit today." Wrap up your comments and leave. Make future contacts by phone.

h) You are going to meet some wonderful, interesting, and challenging children. Plan to have fun, don't try to make calls on a day you feel rushed, and keep your heart open to God's calling and to God's awesome children.

i) If children are visiting with you, be sure they are constantly supervised. Do not take your eyes off them. Recruit other adult help to make sure each child is within sight at all times.

That's it. God bless you!

He Did It! ✑

A friend, whom I had not seen for many years, approached me at a patio party.

"I want to tell you about John," she said. "He often asks about you. He is married and has four children, and they all go to church and are active Christian kids. He wanted me to tell you that."

I could believe it. John was in fourth grade when I knew him. His parents were fine people, worked hard, and contributed to the community in many ways. They had an affiliation with a neighborhood church, but did not attend worship services at that time. I picked up John for Sunday school. He was a great kid, talkative, and interested in everything.

One day, as I was dropped him off at home, John said, "You know, when I grow up and have a family, we are going to go to church every Sunday."

Apparently John did not forget that intention. It's enough to make a Sunday school teacher smile, isn't it?

The Sunday school is the most effective evangelistic tool we have in the church. A large percentage of the members who come to the church on a profession of faith in Jesus Christ come through the Sunday school. I sometimes think of how astonished Sophia Cooke and Robert Raikes would be if they were to visit our modern Sunday schools.

Sophia Cooke began the whole thing by teaching a group of street children to read in the narthex of her father's church over two hundred years ago. When she told Robert Raikes, a newspaperman, about it, he took an immediate interest and gave generous support to the idea of educating children on

Sunday, the only day of the week when they were free from their labor in the mills and factories of England. Robert Raikes felt that an educated populace would be less likely to engage in criminal activity.

By the twenty-first century, Sunday school teachers are among the most numerous of millions of volunteers in our world. Sophia Cooke used the Bible, the book most likely to be present in English homes, to teach reading. The Bible continues to be the text and the inspiration for Christian education.

Today, we know a great deal more about teaching methods, about how people learn, and about how faith is formed and nurtured. Hannah Ball, an early English Methodist, probably provided the first learning tool for Sunday school classes. She painted a series of pictures illustrating Bible stories, and thus gave us our first flip chart. Others began to gather groups of children for learning, using their kitchens, their yards, and sometimes the halls of churches as meeting places.

Often, the parents were more enthusiastic about the classes than the children were. Parents began to understand that their children would have a better life if they learned to read, knew and love Jesus Christ, and avoided the immoral life of the streets. Early writers tell of children brought to the classes by their parents, who would then chain the children's ankles to a log so they couldn't skip class. Robert Raikes and Victor Hugo were among early supporters who brought little cakes and candies to these underprivileged children.

Gradually the idea of the Sunday school spread throughout England, and eventually America. Pastors customarily met midweek with Sunday school teachers to instruct them in the finer points of the lesson for the coming Sunday. National Sunday school conventions became immensely popular. Publishing companies issued a deluge of denominational curriculum materials for all ages, and professional Christian educators were soon found in most of the large churches.

Today, Sunday school teachers have a wide variety of tools to help with their ministry. Curriculum materials, methodologies, rich and interesting settings, training opportunities and ideas, all assist us in doing a better job. I insist that there is no more important task in life than teaching Sunday school, save parenting.

As a farmer, I know that not every seed planted will bear grain. The task, nevertheless, is to continue to plant the seed, and to welcome the harvest with joy and thanksgiving.

One spring my husband and son put in a new pond on our farm for the cattle. I took our small grandchildren with me to help seed the sides of the dam. The back side of the dam, and several feet around the other sides of the pond, were too steep for tractors and seeders, so we put the grass seed in small buckets and walked to and fro, spreading the seed with great sweeps of our arms. As we worked, I told the children the Bible story, pointing out that we were using the same method the Bible man used to seed his fields by hand. We looked for places where the seed might have trouble thriving—around a tree stump, on a clay hill, on a rocky slope.

We talked about Sunday school, about how sometimes we remember the words of Jesus and act in ways that are loving and generous. But sometimes we forget the words of our Lord, and when those seeds do not flourish, we are apt to be selfish and cross. As we trudged wearily back to the house, my little granddaughter slipped her hand into mine.

"Well," she sighed, "I guess most kids don't get to help plant seed, do they?"

Perhaps not. But they do help to plant the seeds of faith as they attend, learn, and love Sunday school. Parents and teachers seize the teachable moment when they plant seeds of caring and justice, when they involve their children in acts of love and mercy, and when they tell the stories of Jesus and help their children to relate to them.

We returned often to the pond that year, and watched as it collected water. We kept a keen eye on our seeding, and the children often compared the growth to what the Bible had to say about the seed of God's word.

And so it was with John. God's word fell on fertile ground with this boy. He resolved early on to be a Christian, to let God's word grow in his life, and to take his family to church. And he did it. Thanks be to God!

What I Learned While Going Out for Pizza

The Junior Highs and I were tooling down the road on the way for pizza after a workday at the church. Dusk was falling as I wheeled the van onto the main highway. We had gone only a mile or so before a shout went up from the back of the van. "Stop, Myrtle! Hey, let's stop! I want that raccoon!"

"You mean that roadkill raccoon?" I asked. "No way."

"C'mon, Myrtle. I want that raccoon!"

"No! I'm not having bloody roadkill in this van. That's one raccoon that will rest in peace, right where he is."

We had a great time and lots of laughs as the kids filled up on pizza. Later, as we were driving back to their small town, one of the girls edged up to the front and asked me quietly if I would please take her home last. This usually meant someone wanted to talk privately, so of course I said yes. The kids were singing and shouting good-bye as each one arrived at his home. Finally, only Marie and I were left in the van.

"You should have stopped for the raccoon," said Marie quietly.

I laughed, not taking her seriously. "Tomorrow I will be the one to tidy up the van. And I don't want to scrub off raccoon blood, believe me!"

"You don't understand," continued Marie. "Bud's parents don't give him lunch money. He has to earn his own, mostly by trapping and selling the hides. A raccoon hide would buy his lunch one day."

I drove back to Bud's house. I told him to bring a plastic sack if he wanted that raccoon, or else plan to clean the van the next day. Bud grinned, grabbed a sack and we headed back down the road.

That roadkill raccoon was gone, but Bud was cheerful about it. "Some other kid must have got it," he said philosophically. He thanked me for the pizza party, thanked me for coming back for him, and said another cheerful goodnight. He never told me he needed that raccoon for lunch money, and I never told him that Marie had sent me back.

How many times do we pass kids, like ships in the night, never knowing what their real intentions or needs are? I suppose Bud could be cheerful about it because it happened so often that he was used to it. In our neighborhood, at least, we don't have many kids who collect roadkill and skin them to sell the hides for lunch money.

Bud made it through high school, went off to Des Moines, and got a good job there in the city. I saw him and his family in a restaurant one Mother's Day. Bud gave me a hug. He had forgotten all about that lost raccoon.

But not me. I continually remind myself to listen to kids. "Hey, stop. I want that raccoon!" could have told me a lot more than I heard. I applaud the sensitivity of Marie, who bothered to correct her teacher, and I applaud Bud, who could remain good humored and friendly, even when I didn't bother to ask why anyone would want a dead raccoon.

There are a lot of raccoons in these beautifully wooded hills of southern Iowa. When they invade our farm buildings, we put out live traps, and then take the captured raccoons to the nearby lake to live the good life there. When I see a dead one on the road, I tell myself to slow my life down, ask the pertinent questions, and keep tuned to the young people around me.

Someone may go without lunch if I fail to listen.

The Jeffs Among Us ⟨≥⟩

Jeff was funny and smart. He was constantly coining words and contriving puns. Overweight, and a little brash, he talked of being an archeologist and of going off to the Middle East to dig up miraculous artifacts. Personally, I expected him to do all those things, and more.

Jeff got along well with adults. Even as a young boy in elementary school, he presented himself with great animation and interest. After high school he enlisted in the army, hoping to have money for college when his enlistment was over. Instead, Jeff found himself facing a discharge from the army on grounds of sexual harassment and sodomy.

Jeff disappeared in Pittsburgh for several years, surfacing only when he faced amputation of a leg. He died of AIDS a few months later. He told his nurses in Pittsburgh that he wanted to go home.

A friend brought his ashes home. We buried him in a nearby cemetery. Jeff had come home. Estranged family members gathered around the urn that held Jeff's ashes. Several old friends and neighbors spoke loving words about Jeff as a boy, about his friendly and cheerful nature. Jeff's journey ended where it began, among those who loved him.

Dallas, on the other hand, was a lean and lanky boy who dropped in at the church a couple times a week. He stopped in every office with a grin, asking what we wanted done today. Sometimes he ran the old hand-cranked mimeograph for the secretary, or carried curriculum materials to classrooms, or tried to teach me how to use the various audiovisual thingam-abobs. Most of the time he gave up on that and simply took the projectors or other equipment to the classrooms where these were to be used on Sunday. He would tell a joke or two, stop in for a conversation with the pastor, then be on his way until Sunday. He never missed Sunday school.

Dallas seemed so self-sufficient. None of us realized at the time that Dallas had a special need to be needed. We liked Dallas and appreciated his helpfulness and his interest in the church.

Dallas died of AIDS a few years after college. Most of his hometown classmates were gone from his by that time, and there was a new pastor as well. His family buried him quietly.

Chuck was something else. He was friendly, but arrogant. He overcompensated. He maneuvered his way past life's difficulties, never owning up to a mistake, but relying on half-truths and misinformation to get his way. He left a trail of exploited and disillusioned public school and Sunday school teachers behind him when he left for New York and hopefully, a career on the stage. Well into his thirties, he is still seeking roles. We all want a better life for Chuck than the one he seems to have settled for.

Sunday school teachers are going to have some homosexual kids in their classes. Some researchers tell us that those with homosexual inclinations may be as many as ten percent of the population. Some will inevitably turn up at Sunday school, thank God.

I do not intend to argue questions of morality, save to ask us all to reserve judgment. We do not yet know all that we need to know about sexual orientation. But we do know the word of Jesus Christ, and that is to love our neighbors. What is Christ's word for Jeff and Dallas and Chuck, and the other gay or lesbian youths who struggle with identity, with the sense of their differentness, with the jeers of their class-mates?

The church cannot abandon the Chucks, the Jeffs, and others with same sex orientation. We are under a mandate to tell the whole world about the love, mercy, and justice that God extends to us through Jesus. The compassion we feel toward these young people is miniscule compared to the compassion of our Lord. How dare we turn away his own?

If we have been judgmental by any turn of phrase, by any overt action, by any omission of love and joy in our friendship, shame on us.

A Safe Place

I was leading a laboratory class in a small church in the west-ern part of our country. A young boy bent over while engrossed in some learning activities, and his t-shirt slipped up, revealing a series of welts across his back. This boy had been beaten, I was sure of it.

When lab school was over, I approached the pastor with what I had observed. My plane left in a few hours, so I requested that he would further investigate and notify offi-cials if this boy had been beaten. Imagine my anger when the pastor refused to have anything to do with it. "His father is head of the trustees," he said. "I can't do anything about this."

I could have decked him.

Many churches are putting safeguards in place to prevent

child molestation. In addition to these preventive steps, however, we must be open to hear what children may be trying to tell us.

In the high school Sunday school class years ago, there were two girls who were "walk-ins" to our church and Sunday school. Every Sunday they remained after class was over. We talked about their schoolwork, their friends, and their interests. However, also hovering near was a boy who insisted on leaving with these girls. He walked the girls to their car. I assumed that he longed to make a good impression on one of them.

One day I read in the newspaper that these girls had gone to the authorities to file charges of incest against their father. They never came back to Sunday school. They were sent to live with relatives in another community after their father was arrested and sentenced.

I'm not sure who had told them they could find help at the church. Weeks of waiting after class should have told me to send the hovering boy away so the girls could share that they needed help. Of course, we cannot be mind readers. We can only be available. Eventually, these girls gave up and went to the civil authorities, which of course is the guidance the church would have offered. But I regret that we missed the signals were not there for them in their difficult decision and action.

Trust me. They are here with us, these boys and girls who need help. We must watch for the signs and heed the warnings. These are children who desire a relationship with God, and who look to us to reflect the love that we love to talk about.

We'll Take You in a Wheelchair

It was an awful Thanksgiving. My husband lay seriously ill in the hospital. After two days at his side, I was exhausted. Our family urged me to return home for a few hours of sleep. "When you come back," they said, "we can go to the cafeteria downstairs for a hamburger."

Returning home, I fell into a deep sleep. Only when whiffs of turkey and dressing invaded the bedroom did I stir enough to wonder where it was coming from. Dragging myself to the kitchen, I found the source—turkey and dressing, potatoes and gravy, salads, everything right down to the pumpkin pie. There was a note also:

"Myrtle: I heard you were going to have a hamburger. So I brought dinner. Love, Stephanie."

After eating a little, I hurried to the hospital to send my family home for the feast while I stayed at my husband's side. No one but Stephanie would think to do this, I marveled.

Stephanie was one of the most complex little girls I ever knew. Blonde with warm brown eyes, she looked like an angel. On the other hand, she was street-smart in ways that I found unbelievable. She knew her rights and legal prerogatives, could argue like a lawyer, and write like a poet. She was some kid.

Now, years later, after a tumultuous youth, Stephanie as parent and friend was still sharing her life with me. I had a lot to be thankful for that Thanksgiving day, in addition to my husband's improving condition.

Stephanie had a large family of older brothers, snapping, barking dogs, and a gorgeous big sister. I remember she came to my house to play only once, and I went to her house only once or twice. Those snarling dogs kept me at a distance. Besides, when I took Stephanie home in the van from the after-school ministries on Monday, she always told me very clearly that I was to let her out at the corner.

Still, Steph and her friend Joyce had plans for me, during all those years of their childhood.

"We are going to live together in a big house with all our children," they declared. "And you can live with us when you get old."

"When I get old, all those children might be too noisy for me," I said.

"Well, then we will make you a room upstairs all by yourself, with lots of books."

"Oh, I don't know. I might get lonely up there all by myself."

With great patience, they countered: "Myrtle. When you get bored, we'll put you in a wheelchair and take you to Ottumwa."

"Okay. It's a deal."

Ottumwa was only fifty miles away, but it seemed pretty big-city to these girls, and I accepted their love and their plans for my old age. Still, there were miles to go before any of us were ready for that.

Stephanie's journey to adulthood led through many-a-snare. She dropped out of high school to have her first baby. Later, she attended an alternative high school and received her high school diploma. All this time Stephanie struggled with her siblings, whom she loved dearly, her parents, and with society in general. She wrote insightful and sensitive poetry—whole notebooks of it—pushed at societal and cultural boundaries, plunged headlong and headstrong into the messes of daily life, and once in a while got overwhelmed by the reality of it all.

She phoned one evening from the mall. "I want you to come. I think I am going to kill myself," she said. Knowing that Stephanie never indulged in half-truths, I asked where I would find her and got in the car.

I never got the details of her despair. I didn't have to. We had been friends a long time by then. Stephanie finally consented to go with me to our pastor's home. Upon his advice and with his help, Stephanie and I drove to a distant hospital that night. Stephanie checked herself in for psychological evaluation.

It didn't get easier, even though Stephanie gained a new understanding of herself and of her worth. She was a wonderful individual, full of creativity. She was a poet on roller skates, a wild bird flying in freedom. I never tried to tether her, only to provide the safe landing places when the air got too thin up where Stephanie was flying. She knew my values. She knew I longed for her to find her way through the tangled path that life had become for her. I kept an even keel and waited for Stephanie's next call.

She had several jobs during those years. She worked in a factory, waited tables, worked as a nurse's aid, and sold cars. She entered into a tempestuous marriage. Finally, she and her husband took her children, his children, and their children and settled into a new community. I received some wonderful letters, frequent emails, and an occasional phone call. Stephanie was happy.

The thing is, this young woman is an awesome mother! She and her husband, who have found some peace in their marriage in a new community, have sensible family rules and stand for little nonsense. Steph does the usual soccer mom stuff, has seen her daughter through her high school years and into college, and still has a house full of boys. She and her oldest daughter have joined a church. Stephanie is not active, to my sorrow, but her daughter has been active in the youth program and looks forward to her church activities.

I often reflect back on the years we have shared. "I made a lot of mistakes," Stephanie says. "But you never judged me and never gave up on me."

I asked Stephanie if her Monday school years had an impact on her life.

"Monday school brought me a sense of togetherness. Even the 'mean' kids gave it up for a bit every Monday, just to come together at church and have fun. Some came for the stories, some for the neat activities, and some just for the snack. I watched my teacher give a box of food here and there to families that could use a little boost, and that helped me to know how Christian people help one another. Then later on, while helping you to teach Monday school when I was in high school, I learned how great it was to see a new generation of kids still coming and learning together, as well as treating each other as equals and as friends.

"At school everyone broke into groups and you had the kids who wouldn't play with other certain children. But at Monday school, no one cared who was wearing the right clothes or the wrong shoes. Everyone was just friends. Our teachers just showed us how Christians behave with each other, and we grew to like each other.

"I loved singing with everyone and could never wait until the next Monday after school to do it all again. For some of the kids it was a safe haven where they felt protected for at least a little while before having to go home to whatever turbulence they may have had in their lives. It was a break from the screaming, fighting, and in some cases abuse for a lot of children."

In retrospect, I often ponder my relationship with Stephanie. It has been more than teacher, more than friend. She has been my "mentee" I have loved, supported, advised, and suggested. There have been times when I would like to boss her around a little, but usually my respect for her and her innate good sense kept me from it. In her mature years we have worked together with children, shared problems, talked about our values and our faith.

We still mull over the problems with which the children in our communities are struggling. Steph brings a perspective to situations that I do not possess, and I bring years of experience with children that can have a bearing on our discussions. Together we tackle a lot.

It's comforting to know that in the end, when I am very old, I will have a nice room at Stephanie's house, and she will take me to Ottumwa in a wheelchair when I get bored.

What Curriculum?

"It won't work," said my young friend Eric. We were sitting at a picnic table in the town park, going over our vacation Bible school papers for the day. Eric was studying a picture of a watershed, which looked okay to me. "God, the Universe and Me" was a great study as far as I was concerned.

"Why not?" I asked. This sixth grade class was sharp. Besides, Eric was a farm boy who had been around the land all his short life. Maybe Eric knew something I didn't.

"Ask Paul," he responded. "But I don't think it is right."

I took the paper home that day to my husband Paul, a farmer whose knowledge of the land far exceeds my own. He looked at it intently for a moment before he said, "It won't work."

Okay. I wrote the publishing company a note about the picture. But by then I had another matter to consider.

"If I'd known Bible school was just paper work," said Eric, "I would have stayed home to sheer sheep." This kid was not a smart aleck. He was a serious farm boy who had daily, serious responsibilities at home. All my experiences as a Sunday school teacher told me that I must adapt any written curriculum materials to meet the needs of the students, but here I was sitting at a picnic table in a lovely park filling out blanks in a printed student paper, while this boy could be sheering sheep.

I put away the papers. The rest of the week, the kids and I went on field trips. We picked up trash on the roads and ditches leading to that small town. We visited a History Farm that showed us farms from the time of the Native Americans to the present day. We visited a conservationist who explained how ponds, streams, and farming practices in our area were related to the natural watershed. An amateur astrologer set up his equipment in our farm meadow and helped us to identify stars. The class had enough ideas to provide us with an exciting (and exhausting!) week of learning about God's amazing creation.

Yes, we learned a few Bible verses in the van as we made our way to these places of interest. One musical fellow taught us some camp songs as well. We prayed for safe journeys and for God to add wisdom to our knowledge, and we all grew in our awareness of the presence of Jesus Christ. Especially the teacher.

What a gift sixth graders are! Even though their hostilities, identity problems, and emerging hormones can occasionally be disruptive, we can value their forthrightness, their quirky humor, their energy, curiosity, and creativity. How exciting to be a part of a sixth grader's life!

I am continually pleased and gratified by the spiritual seeking so evident in most pre-teens. One said to me this week, "I want to take confirmation class now. I don't understand where God came from."

A kindergarten boy approached me on the sidewalk outside church, accompanied by his Dad. "If God made dinosaurs, how come we don't still have 'em?"

Another responded to my water-steam-ice explanation of the Trinity. "It makes sense with material stuff. But didn't you say God is Spirit? I don't get it."

Another shared, "I want to pray about my folks' divorce, but I can't pray. It doesn't come out right." When I suggested that we just be silent and receptive for a moment, knowing that the Holy Spirit would pray for us in troubled times, he seemed appreciative but apprehensive.

What was going on here?

John Westerhoff, in his book *Will Our Children Have Faith?* (New York: Morehouse Group, 2000), has given us some guidelines. Westerhoff illustrates faith development by means of a series of circles. He describes the first and smallest circle as a stage of experiential faith. This is always the beginning of the journey, no matter what our age. It is the experience we have of God's presence with us, whether as a baby being lovingly cared for by parents, or as an elderly person who may see God's presence in life for the first time.

The second stage is the affiliate. We know God through our relationships with Christian parents, church family, Sunday school, choir, or adult small groups. We exchange experiences, grow in love toward each other and toward God, and accept Jesus as our friend and redeemer. We may not live out a close, personal relationship with our Lord, but we grow toward that ideal.

Most preteens and teenagers are in the third circle, if their Christian community has nurtured them. This is a time of searching, of questioning, and of examining the faith to which they have been exposed. Some people never grow out of the experiential or affiliative stages, and that is okay. As Westerhoff says, his circles are like the growth rings of a tree. No matter how many circles there are, a tree is a tree. No matter which circle of faith you embrace, faith is faith. Most of us seek and question all our lives, even as we move into an "owned faith," a relationship with Jesus and a theological perspective upon which we base our whole lives. We know that God is guiding our journey, and that God can intervene in our faith experiences at any time.

With these understandings in mind, teachers do not reject questions, or even doubts. The kindergarten boy who needs to know about dinosaurs is seeking, just as the junior high grieving over his parents' divorce is. God is present in all the questions, and we teachers had better not duck the tough ones.

We share our own faith stories, our own times of questions and uncertainty, our own mountain top experiences of God, and our own prayers for wisdom and grace. Sometimes we push the student to think deeper, to articulate clearer, and to let go and let God. Most of all, we encourage these young people. We partner with them as we engage in life's biggest questions and most important decisions.

Our best curriculum is always the curriculum that deals with the inner person and with the spiritual quest of the student. I am dedicated to printed curriculum materials that are based on age level needs, Biblical scholarship, and sound theology. But I am also dedicated to the Erics who might as well be sheering sheep as filling out blanks. My dedication to Eric means that I must go where he is, puzzle where he puzzles, explore where he explores, and eventually watch Eric as he takes his own path to Jesus Christ.

The Little Girl Who Saved a Church

She was only seven years old when her Aunt June invited her to Sunday school. It didn't occur to her to wonder why she was the only child there, nor that there were only eight people in worship that morning. She just knew she liked it. A nice teacher showed her where the children had Sunday school. She loved hearing the Bible story and quickly learned the memory verse, colored a picture, and began a project with her teacher. Lydia didn't know it, and neither did that small congregation, but that day began a long and enduring love affair between Lydia and her church.

Lydia, now a beautiful, active young woman in high school and church, says, "I am what I am today because of that Sunday school." The folks at Lydia's church add, "The church is what it is today because of Lydia."

You see, Lydia thought the whole experience of Sunday school was so great that she kept asking her friends to go with her. At first, it was only one or two. Then she asked a family with six children, all of whom agreed that Sunday school was, indeed, a fine thing to do on Sunday. They learned that Jesus loved them. "The people there made us feel special," says Lydia.

We all know the story of Lydia's first Easter in church. When her older sisters suggested that the family celebrate Easter by going with their Grandmother to her church, Lydia told her family, "You can go to Grandmother's church, but I am going to my church."

That did it. Lydia's family all went with Lydia to her church, where everyone was made to feel special and loved on this Christian holy day. Lydia's sisters and her parents decided they would join Lydia and her Aunt June in becoming active, committed members of Lydia's small congregation. By the next Easter morning, Lydia had invited almost all of her wide extended family to join her. There were eighty people in church that morning, the most this congregation had seen in decades. Baptisms, confirmation classes, and adult professions of faith began to happen regularly.

Of course all this required some changes. One new member put his professional skills to work in overseeing the waterproofing, renovation, and painting of the basement area of the church building. Some women with decorating skills added plants, paintings, and other accessories. These updates made the kitchen look frowsy, so the whole group undertook to modernize the kitchen. Then they decided to build a ramp for ease of entrance to the church, and establish a new office with modern office equipment.

A new pastor, a young woman with lots of energy and a great love for children, worked with the children and youth in new programs. A long-time member, one who had faithfully committed her time and talents to the congregation even when it was struggling with only eight members, brought records up to date, assisted the pastor in calling and teaching, and began training as a certified lay missioner.

Lydia continued her inviting. She greeted people at the door and gave out hymnbooks and bulletins. She loved the Christmas programs and the occasions when her pastor took the whole youth group to other churches in her charge to help with worship. Once Lydia led the whole worship service by herself, an awesome day in Lydia's life.

By the time Lydia was twelve years old, her congregation acknowledged her as an evangelist. They submitted a nomination to her annual conference when it honored evangelistic efforts. Lydia won this honor as a Youth Evangelist.

"I didn't know what was happening," Lydia said. "I thought I might have to answer questions in front of everyone or give a speech or something. The congregation wanted it to be a surprise, so I didn't know when I went to Annual Conference that day that it was already decided that I was Youth Evangelist for the year. I was totally surprised, for sure.

"Ever since I heard the story of Lydia and how she helped the apostle Paul in the Bible, I have felt that I can help, too. My favorite color is purple!"

Lydia continues to be active in many areas of life. She enjoys sports at her high school, shows her horse at the county fair, participates in 4-H activities, plays her horn in the high school band, sings in chorus, enjoys her church and home, and helps to teach the children in her Sunday school.

"I want to be an orthodontist," she says. As a child Lydia had years of orthodontal treatment. "They even broke my jaw to make room for all my teeth," she laughs. "I want to help other kids to have healthy teeth and a good smile."

Lydia's experience is a classic example of the connection between Christian education and evangelism. Faith is a wonderful gift of God, and a congregation that loved and valued her nurtured Lydia in her faith. Lydia's experience in reaching out to the children of her small town was truly a response to faith, an act of living out the will of God for her life. Most congregations interpret "child evangelism" to mean the various ways in which we reach out to children so they may know the love of God, the saving power of Jesus the Christ, and the ongoing presence of the Holy Spirit in their lives and in the life of the church.

In the life of faith, child evangelism may mean, as it does in Lydia's case, the impact that a deeply committed child may have on those around her. How often we hear the statement, "get the children to church, and the adults will come with them"?

Maybe.

I have known just as many cases where the adults *send* the children to Sunday school, but make no effort to *bring* them. Children certainly can be enthusiastic evangelists, given some leadership and guidance by their Sunday school teachers and other adults.

If you are looking to increase your efforts in the area of evangelism, here are a few ways to begin:

Provide the opportunity for children to be in ministry with adults in every work area of the church. Children can help with mission projects, contribute ideas in Christian education projects, and evangelize through word of mouth with their peers.

One Sunday school class made bright door hangers from poster board. When our church moved to a new part of town, the message on the door hangers read, "Hi, Neighbor! We are new in the neighborhood. Please come to a hot dog feast at our picnic shelter and get acquainted." We added the date and time, and then the children decorated the door hangers with markers, beads, sequins, and stickers. A week before the picnic the teachers and their classes divided up the neighborhood and rang the doorbell at every house. The children greeted those who were home, and hung a door hanger invitation where there was no answer to our ring. We kept everything simple (hot dogs and watermelon) so that the children could help serve and still have plenty of time for water balloon volleyball and other summer games with new friends from the neighborhood. Whatever the special occasion in your church, the children can help prepare and make it a comfortable place for visiting children.

Don't waste those student take-home papers! Ask children to deliver the papers to absentees, if possible. Other leftovers may be taken to children in the hospital, non-churched families, and playmates in the neighborhood. As a teacher, I keep a couple of student papers folded in my purse. I sometimes see youngsters with their parents at the dentist or doctor's office, irritable children in the grocery store, or tired children in other public places where I can ask the parent if it is okay to give the child a paper to look at. I have never been refused! Children can share in this way with each other as well.

Encourage children to tell others the stories of Jesus. A knot of elementary girls was talking earnestly in one corner of the playground. One child broke away to approach the playground supervisor. "Well!" she said indignantly, hands on her hips, "You would think someone could have told *me* about God!"

Thank God the other children saw that as important. That indignant little girl came to an after-school Bible class for several years as a result of her conversation on the playground.

The older elementary class in our church was studying a unit of curriculum on love. We teachers began to question our effectiveness when we discovered that these kids were by no means practicing love in school, to each other, or to anyone else. We decided what we really needed was a ninety percent learning activity. Children retain approximately ten percent of what they hear alone, but approximately ninety percent of what they learn through purposeful activity.

We knew of a physically challenged woman in a nearby neighborhood who lived alone with her ninety-year-old mother. These women lived in a home heated by a wood stove, and it seemed a loving thing to saw firewood to take to her home during these fierce winter days. Several fathers came to saw the wood. The kids loaded it into the pickup truck, and we all went to their home.

One of the fathers knocked at the door. When Alice saw the load of wood, she burst into tears. "Where do you want us to put it?" asked my friend.

"Oh, just unload it there by the sidewalk," replied Alice.

"These strong kids can do better than that. We'll put it in the woodshed for you." Al stepped back and opened the door of the woodshed.

A small pile of cobs from the summer sweet corn and another pile of walnut shells were all that were in the woodshed. A silent bunch of kids began to unload the wood. One boy carried an armload into the house to fuel a faltering fire in the wood stove, around which an aged woman hovered.

Afterwards, we went to the church for cookies and hot chocolate. As we began to talk about our experience, recognizing that these good women had been without any more wood for the fire on this frigid winter day, one of the boys asked, "Myrtle, do you think God sent us?"

What do you think? Let's ask Lydia. Her church would undoubtedly say, "Yes! God does sometimes send kids to do God's work."

God Has a Purpose for Me ✍

"Salt and pepper! Salt and pepper!" The chant greeted Twyla and Tracy as they boarded the school bus. The sisters grinned as they took their seats, even though Twyla secretly hid the hurt in her heart. You see, Twyla was black, and her sister Tracy was white. Though the kids in town all ran around with one another, playing ball in the ball park, roller skating on the cement slab in the middle of the two-block downtown area, sliding on the hills of town right after a snowfall, Twyla always felt a little different from the other kids.

Twyla and Tracy understood that they had different fathers, but Twyla never understood why her mother would not tell her about her father. She wouldn't even tell her his name. Now a mother with her own children, Twyla knows nothing about her natural father.

"It is a small cloud between me and my mother," acknowledges Twyla. "I wouldn't interrupt his life. He doesn't know about me. It would just be nice to know that I have a father someplace."

Twyla and Tracy sometimes came to the small church on the hill to worship with their grandmother when they were small. When their mother was hired to clean the church building, the girls heard for the first time about Monday school. There they participated in games, snacks, Bible films and stories, drama, music, and much conversation with caring Christian adults. Twyla loved it from the start.

A gangly little girl, Twyla was strong and agile. Though she hid her hurts and sometimes seemed shy, she was popular with the other kids. "Besides," she chuckles today, "Tracy was more aggressive than I was, and Tracy didn't put up with much. She stuck up for me when I was a kid, every step of the way."

As the girls entered junior and senior high school, we saw less of them at church, particularly after their grandmother died. "Mom was busy with a boy friend," explains Twyla. "She didn't go to church."

Twyla had a coach who believed in her, or so she thought. Active in volleyball, basketball, and softball, Twyla was growing into a fine athlete. She dreamed of excelling, of winning athletic scholarships that would make college possible, and of earning lasting friendship with the kids with whom she had grown up in her desperate little town.

"I was good," she acknowledges. "I worked very hard on my sports."

Twyla vividly remembers the awful day when she was a senior in high school. "I went to my coach seeking understanding," she says. "I had to tell him that I was pregnant." Her coach was appalled. He offered to pay for an abortion. He did not want to lose such a fine player on his teams, and right before conference finals at that.

Here was this fatherless girl, still seeking her own identity, asked to put an end to the life of her child. Twyla knew she could not do this. She withdrew from all sports, finished out her senior year, gave birth to a darling little boy, and found work as a clerk in a local store. Her coach no longer even spoke to her. This was not the stuff of big dreams.

Twyla worked at several jobs over the next year or so. It is not easy to be a single mother with a baby needing attention and a poverty-level job. When a friend suggested that she apply for a job in Missouri where she could work filing patient records for a dentist while receiving training as a dental assistant, Twyla leaped at the opportunity. It was soon evident that Twyla was skilled at this job. She was quick to understand and respond as an assistant, cheerful and comfortable with patients, strong, and capable of working hours on her feet. Twyla was happy and confident that she had found her niche.

Twyla says, "I always lived in the white community. I had no connection with the black community at all. No one in the black community ever acknowledged me or recognized me as black. Most people just forget about it."

During the next year, Twyla met a man whom she loved dearly. They lived together for years before Twyla discovered, just weeks before giving birth to their little girl, that he had been having an affair with another woman and had, in fact, married her. Twyla was devastated. Now without a job, without a home, eight months pregnant, and with a four-year-old to care for, Twyla felt very much alone in the world. Back in their hometown, her sister Tracy had married and had a family of her own. Twyla felt that things were grim.

At that point a saintly lady who lived nearby offered to take her in. This neighbor, who had an extra room in her home, offered Twyla security and comfort, and her babies safety and love. "I was heartbroken," says Twyla. "I made it because of her."

Twyla once more drew on her innate strength and faith. "I knew God had a purpose for me and for my children. I went to work for another dentist nearer home. I found housing for my children and myself. I put my little boy in school, and we mended our lives."

One day a few years later, I walked into my dentist's office and found a familiar, smiling face as Twyla waited to drape the napkin around my neck. I had no idea where she had been in those years following high school. We have shared many a memory and many a chuckle since then.

Twyla is married now. Her husband is a loving, caring, Christian man. "He is older than I am," says Twyla, "but we are happy, and he is a wonderful father to my children. He built a house for us on a hill by a lovely lake. The children are in school. Tyler is great at math and sports; Drew is a reader, an introspective little girl. We go the church together. Life is good for us."

I asked Twyla if Monday school had affected her life in any way.

> "What I remember most is my teacher. She loved me, and told me that God loved me. Monday school gave direction to my whole life. God has been with me. I have certainly made some mistakes, but I have always known that God has a purpose for me and for my children. Family is everything to me. I want my children to know Jesus and to find God's direction for their own lives. Together, my husband Harry and I will try to do this right."

Often, people have told me that they don't remember the particular things they did in Sunday school or Monday school, but they remember how they felt. Some remember the Bible stories or activities, particularly if they have had follow-up and support from parents, but almost every child will remember if he or she felt accepted, loved, and valued.

When the Sunday school classroom most resembles a school experience, children are more likely to feel indifferent to it. When the Sunday school environment is informal and inviting, the relationships friendly, accepting, and loving, and the activities geared to the children's social and spiritual needs, they are more likely to know Jesus and to remember the enduring truths of the Bible as they live them out with their classmates and teachers.

Jesus himself did not have a classroom, or even a class space. He taught adults in the synagogue, but his contacts with children as recorded in the Gospels were always in a comfortable, familiar setting. He blessed the children and cautioned the disciples not to forbid them to come to him as he conversed by the lake and beside the pathways.

Twyla exhibited courage and resilience in her growing-up years. Her faith was nurtured in her grandmother's church, and in a Monday school where she was loved. She returned to that little church to be married, and today her whole family attends a small church in a town near the lake. Twyla has forgiven the people who abandoned her, both spiritually and physically, and is resolved to give stability and love to her children.

Today, Twyla and I exchange memories of the kids we knew, the town where she grew up, the Monday school where we knew each other as beloved children of God. It almost makes going to the dentist easy, just to see Twyla.

A Twelve-Rabbit Morning

Randy and his sister lived at the end of a long lane leading from a small country road. I wheeled the parish van up that long lane, past a field of sweet clover, past Randy's mother's luxurious garden, verdant with vegetables, to pick up the children for vacation Bible school. Randy always occupied the seat of honor in the van. He rode shotgun in the front seat, alerting me to the many rabbits that hopped and jumped along that long lane. We certainly didn't want to ruin our day by running over a rabbit! From the time he was a very little boy, Randy counted the scampering rabbits as we headed for his little country church.

Randy loved announcing "It's a six-rabbit morning!" or "It's a ten-rabbit morning!" as the teachers and other children at Bible school cheered. Eventually, whenever something seemed very special someone would exclaim, "Wow! This is a ten-rabbit morning!"

That little church had a lot of ten-rabbit mornings at Sunday school. I began to ponder why this was so. I began to list what every Sunday school teacher should know in order to have a ten-rabbit morning with the students. The list includes everything, of course. But since that is hardly possible, let's list a few of the essentials.

An effective Sunday school teacher knows God as Creator and loving Parent, Jesus as Christ and Redeemer, the Holy Spirit as God Present. Sure in her or his faith, and living a personal life of devotion, effective teachers attends worship services as an expression of Christian discipline and an opportunity for corporate praise. This teacher is sure to have an impact on students. You just can't hide a real Christian spirit, nor should you want to.

That paragraph is loaded, by the way. It doesn't mean one has no questions. Most of us have a number of them, but those questions never doubt the person of God in the midst of human life, or the saving power of Jesus the Christ. We nurture our questions. They are the stuff of our prayers, our thoughts, and our conversations with intimate friends. We share appropriate questions with our students, encouraging them to think, consider their own experiences, and reach out to others for enlightenment. Perhaps such early classroom experiences will help our students to be respectful of others' convictions, while at the same time keep their own learning edges sharp and receptive.

Effective teachers attend worship and urge their students to do so also. A three-year-old stood beside me during worship, singing away with his hymnbook upside down. I leaned over to hear his words.

"Hallelujah, Hallelujah, we shall be hungry nevermore, Hallelujah, Hallelujah, we shall be hungry nevermore," sang this little boy.

I'm not sure whether this boy didn't have breakfast, or whether he was just looking forward to lunch, but I know for sure that he knew what was happening in church: We were praising God. Hallelujah!

It may be a temptation to leave before worship after a busy morning in Sunday school, but believe me, both children and their parents are very aware of what we do. (God is too.) And we do want children in worship. They are a part of the Body of Christ, and to exclude them from worship is to deny the gift.

Effective teachers must know their way through the Bible with ease, familiarity, and affection. We do not worship the Bible, but we worship God and know God's truths are contained in the Bible. Our respect for God's Word is evident to every child.

Todd was always a delight to me. He cherished the Bible given to him in the third grade. He kept it in its box, brought it to Sunday school, and during worship he often sat in the balcony, where he carefully extracted his Bible from the box and read the Scripture along with the pastor.

The Bible is so rich that no teacher can attain to the knowledge of everything that is in it. However, we can study until we know the basic facts about the Bible: how many books, which are Hebrew Scriptures and which are New Testament, the sweep of Israelite history, other types of literature in the Bible, the stories of Jesus, and the Easter event.

We open ourselves to the Scriptures by asking ourselves three questions: *What* did this verse or section say to the people of that time, *so what* does it say to me today, and *now what* am I expected to do. God speaks to us in such personalized study, and we grow as teachers as our hearts are drawn to God.

The effective teacher knows his or her students, and as far as possible, knows their life situation. The effective teacher knows that Stacy's cousin "drownded in the crik" last night, that Josh jumped from the roof of the house and almost broke his neck, that Lydia is a finalist in the Miss Teenage Pageant.

Of course that is not always possible, but it becomes more nearly so if the teacher has visited the home of every one of his or her current students. If we have made an effort to become acquainted with every parent, if we have allowed time in the class for sharing, if sometimes we gather for informal hours of fun, food and planning, then we begin to know things. Let the children identify a need and plan how to act together to be God's missionaries. We allow quiet times when Jesus truly enters the hearts of our children.

To know God through Jesus Christ, to know the Bible, to know the students: —what else would we need? A nice classroom helps. But I have taught in a furnace room painted pink, and I have taught on the floor of the high school hallway as we worshipped there while awaiting our new church building. I have taught in a very fine classroom. But in every case, the real teaching and learning happens when both the children and I seek to know God better, to understand our Bible better, and to love each other more.

That makes for a *twelve*-rabbit morning, right?